Dedication

Continue to rest my sweet mother in law Hannah Adiele Nlewem

My loving husband Dr. Chimezie Nlewem

My beautiful children Chinedu, Chidera, Chiemezie, and Chigozie.

My parents Mr. &. Mrs. Lawrence Jefferson

My sister Teashayll Jefferson-Lee

Cousin Lisa Smith

The festival serves as a way to celebrate the successful yam harvest, which is a staple crop in many West African communities. Yam is considered a vital food source and a symbol of prosperity, so the festival allows people to rejoice in the abundance of the harvest.

Nigeria's Independence day is October 1 of every year.

"At Christmas, we come together and celebrate with festivals," said to Chidera's father.

Chidera sits down with her father for a thoughtful conversation about Igbo culture. She's curious and eager to learn more about their roots.

Chidera starts by asking her father, "Daddy, where is Igbo land?" Her father shows her a map and explains that Igbo land is located in southeastern Nigeria, a region known for its lush landscapes and vibrant culture.

Chidera is intrigued and asks, "Who are the Igbo people?" Her father describes how the Igbo people are a diverse and resilient group with a rich history. He tells her about their traditions, values, and strong sense of community.

Chidera's curiosity continues as she asks, "What language do we speak?" Her father explains that the Igbo people speak the Igbo language, one of the most widely spoken languages in Nigeria. He encourages Chidera to learn and appreciate their native tongue.

'What language do we speak?'

Chidera's father shares stories about Igbo customs and traditions, from the New Yam Festival to the importance of extended families. Chidera listens attentively, gaining a deeper understanding of their cultural heritage.

"Chidera learns about Igbo customs and traditions."

Chidera expresses her desire to learn more about Igbo culture and carry their traditions forward. Her father smiles proudly, knowing that Chidera's curiosity and passion will help preserve their heritage.

As their conversation continues, Chidera and her father bond over their shared love for Igbo culture. Together, they embark on a journey of discovery and appreciation for their roots.

The end, but the start of a lifelong connection to Igbo culture. Chidera's heart is filled with a deep sense of belonging, and she's excited to explore and celebrate their heritage together.

"The end, but the start of a lifelong connection to Igbo culture."

Thank you for joining Chidera on her cultural exploration! Remember, learning about your culture and heritage is a beautiful way to connect with your roots and build a strong sense of identity. Embrace the richness of your heritage!

Author

Zorena Nlewem is an educator who loves her Nigerian culture. Nlewem truly enjoys giving back to her community. She is married with four children. She is originally from Virginia but currently resides in Georgia. Zorena believes that every child should have the opportunity to escape into a world of wonder through the magic of storytelling. With her books, she aims to ignite a love for reading, nurture creativity, and promote kindness and empathy among young readers. When she's not busy dreaming up new adventures, Zorena enjoys going to the beach or traveling with her family and friends. Join Zorena on a journey through her imaginative tales, and let the magic of her words light up your world and fill your heart with wonder and joy.